This is the third in our series applying different disciplines to the content of RE. It examines theology and natural sciences, focusing on the contributions of both of those disciplines to our thinking about the natural world.

The resource offers clear accounts of those two disciplines, with Investigator Files written by our experts, Dr Alexander Hall (environmental science, pp. 22–23) and Dr Simeon Zahl (theology – Resource 4.1 online). It provides case studies from four environmental charities, including secular and Sikh examples (pp. 4–7). The book includes eight perspectives on the relationship between humans and nature – voices from atheist Humanist via Buddhist and Pagan to ethical vegan (pp. 8–11 and Resource 3.3 online).

The creation account in Genesis has been influential in western thought and we examine it in some detail, offering perspectives from the first to the twenty-first centuries (pp. 16–19), and exploring concepts of dominion and stewardship (pp. 14–15). Practical scenarios on rising sea levels alert students to the work of environmental science (pp. 28–31 and Resource 9.3 online). Students bring their theological learning to bear as they consider the extent that science can guide on what choices to take, once the data is in. Students use nature documentaries to analyse the potentially prophetic role of popular science and scientists (pp. 32–33).

The focus on the environment is important, not least because climate change is such a pressing existential crisis, of great concern to students. This resource supports students' learning about religious attitudes towards and responses to the environment; it offers clarity on how theological and scientific knowledge differ and relate; and it encourages students to reflect on how their own personal worldviews affect their ways of seeing and responding to the natural world.

Stephen Pett, Editor

Conte

1 Diving in: studying religion and science

Introducing religion and science

The relationship between religion and science is a common topic in religious education (RE). It often involves looking at cosmology, evolution and questions of origins, setting up the range of potential relationships with the Genesis creation story. Dominant narratives of the relationship include:

- the conflict or epistemic model (science vs religion as two opposing forms of knowledge)
- the 'non-overlapping magisteria' or NOMA model, from Stephen Jay Gould (science and religion occupy different domains – asking 'how?' and 'why?' questions, for example)
- the hydraulic model (similar to the conflict model, but incorporating an extra element: as religiosity increases acceptance of science decreases and vice versa)
- a model of integration (suggesting that science and religion represent complementary and compatible positions).

This book looks to examine some differences and connections between religion and science. It is not focusing on the theoretical idea of the various models outlined above. Instead, it looks to engage students more practically by applying the disciplines of theology and environmental science (as an example of a natural science). By getting students using the disciplines, they will recognise the different ways of knowing that they represent, and also learn to evaluate these ways of knowing appropriately.

Theology makes some assumptions about the existence of God, generally starting with agreement that God exists, although this is not universally held by theologians. It explores the nature and character of God, as revealed within key texts often regarded as sacred revelations from God. In Christianity, for example, the Bible is commonly the basis for teachings, doctrines and codes for living within Christian traditions and institutions. It underpins ongoing discussion and conversations as Christians address philosophical questions and engage with their contemporary situations through the ages, such as when thinking about creation and the environment. Theology also involves philosophical reasoning – thinking logically and coherently about religious ideas.

The natural sciences start from a different perspective. They focus on describing and understanding natural processes and the world around us. They do this through measuring and observing nature, and placing the information gained into theories and frameworks that help us to understand, explain and predict how the natural world works. The sciences use a general method that involves *observation* that leads to a question; proposing a *hypothesis*; *experimentation* to test the hypothesis; *analysing* the data gathered; and drawing *conclusions* of the experiments in relation to the hypothesis.

By focusing on the environment, this book allows students to practise theological skills of textual analysis, philosophical reasoning and ethical application. They have the opportunity to see how the scientific method leads to data and theories – but at this point there is debate as to whether science should prescribe action and demand it. By trying out a range of scenarios relating to the climate crisis, students get to examine how far religious perspectives might help guide actions.

Teaching and learning approach

As with the other books in this series, the resources in *Studying Religion and the Environment* seek to enable teachers and students to look *through* a range of disciplinary lenses at the substantive content of religious and non-religious worldviews, and also to look *at* these disciplinary lenses or methods. A third purpose is to open students' eyes to the lenses that they are already wearing as they look at the world – to recognise that they encounter the content of RE from within their own worldviews, and to become aware of how that shapes their own understanding and their responses.

Teaching and learning approach: Rob Freathy's summary suggests a three-strand approach, where RE explores the: **Object of study, Methods of study and Subject.**

These three strands can be discerned behind the approaches that follow in this series.

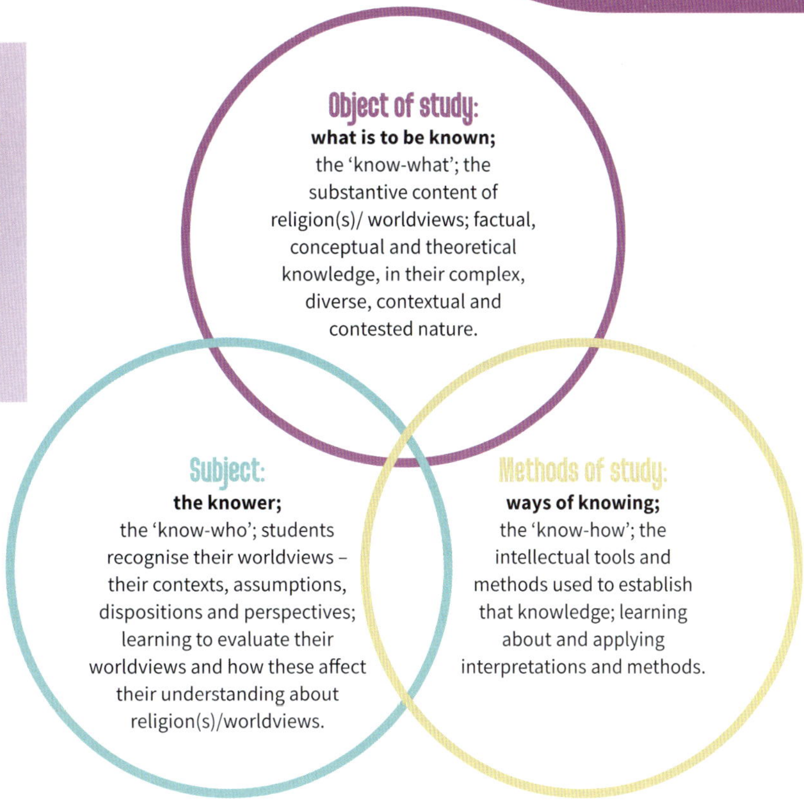

Kinds of knowledge

This book distinguishes between 'substantive' knowledge and 'disciplinary' knowledge. These terms are increasingly present in educational discourse, although they are not consistently applied. In these books, **substantive knowledge** concerns the subject content being studied, in terms of the core concepts, truth claims, teachings and practices of traditions (mainly religious, but applying to non-religious worldviews too), and the behaviour and responses of adherents within traditions, noting that boundaries may be blurred and that much of this knowledge is contested. **Disciplinary knowledge** concerns the methods by which the substantive knowledge is reached. For example, this book explores: how theology uses textual analysis and philosophical reasoning to examine the relationships between God, the Earth and humanity; and how environmental scientists gather data through experiment, recognising that the decisions on what actions to take as a result of the data require the input of other disciplines and communities.

Before you start

This resource heeds the call from Pearce et al (2021) to take care over how we handle questions of religion and science in RE. We have tried to follow their recommendation that RE should 'contextualise relationships between religion and science in new areas that … draw the focus away from easy assumptions of a binary choice' (Pearce, 187). The context of the climate crisis allows students to appreciate the way in which science can provide invaluable data about how the world is, while the kinds of theological, ethical and moral reflections undertaken in religious traditions encourage and enable thinking about values, principles, purposes and meanings that go beyond the data.

Read their research paper in **BJRE**: Jo Pearce, Alexis Stones, Michael J. Reiss & Tamjid Mujtaba (2021) '"Science is purely about the truth so I don't think you could compare it to non-truth versus the truth." Students' perceptions of religion and science, and the relationship(s) between them: religious education and the need for epistemic literacy', *British Journal of Religious Education*, 43:2, 174–189, **doi.org/10.1080/01416200.2019.1635434**

Follow up with a look at the brilliant work of the **Epistemic Insight** project – essential theoretical and practical help for handling religion and science in the classroom: **www.epistemicinsight.com**

Revisit the ***REtoday*** magazine from Autumn 2020: Vol. 38 No. 1 – a rich source of substantive content and teaching and learning inspiration on climate justice: **retodaylibrary.org.uk**

On the subject of the relationship between science and religion, if you haven't seen the excellent comic ***My Evolution*** by Jordan Collver, relating to the work of the Science and Belief in Society project at Birmingham University, you must address that immediately: **sciencereligionspectrum.org/in-the-news/my-evolution-living-along-the-spectrum-of-science-and-religion/**

STUDENT 11–13

2 CASE STUDIES: who cares for the environment, and how?

Case studies: who cares for the environment, and how?

Teaching and learning activities

Resource 2.

These pages offer case studies of four organisations that care for the environment – three religious and one secular. Online, there are teaching and learning ideas, to help you think through what these groups do and why.

Case study 1: Friends of the Earth

Friends of the Earth is an organisation that campaigns to look after the planet.

Aims: Friends of the Earth is committed to:

- **A peaceful and sustainable world**: everyone depends on the planet, so we need to live in harmony with nature to keep it in good shape.
- **A better environment for all**, with a safer climate and healthy air, water and food, as a healthy planet is one that works for people too.
- **An active diverse network** of people acting together for a flourishing, sustainable and socially just environment, acting together for the planet and everyone who lives on it.

Origins: The organisation started in San Francisco, USA, in 1971. At first it aimed to stop the use of nuclear energy. It has grown its work to campaign about many issues to do with looking after the environment.

Image: oleschwander / Shutterstock.com

Campaigns: Friends of the Earth …

… was successful in 1971 at getting big companies to make glass bottles recyclable

… has campaigned to Save the Whale since the 1970s

… protested against cutting down rainforest hardwoods like mahogany to use in UK furniture

… helped people to learn in the 1990s that toxic emissions in the air were causing acid rain

… campaigned to get the government to help older people, and the planet of course, by insulating homes better

… led the campaign to bring a recycling box and a collection to every home in the UK – which became law in 2003

… joined with over 500 other groups like Christian Aid, Islamic Relief, the Royal College of Nursing and Comic Relief to Make Poverty History

… helped protect bees in the UK by introducing National Pollinator Plans and banning bee-harming

… is fighting to stop the plans for a third runway at Heathrow Airport

… is determined to double tree cover in the UK

… is still fighting global climate change.

Friends of the Earth campaigns in 70 countries. In the UK, it has lots of local groups and thousands of supporters who join in its campaigns. It works with lots of other organisations, businesses, politicians and other leaders.

- It is looking to get people to use new, renewable, sources of energy (not coal or petrol).
- It wants to find smarter ways of feeding the world's population without trashing the planet.
- It hopes to find ways to make cities work better, to protect the environment, not damage it.

Links: **friendsoftheearth.uk**

Case study 2: IFEES/EcoIslam

The Islamic Foundation for Ecology and Environmental Sciences is a charity that works to maintain a healthy Earth.

Origins: IFEES began in the mid-1980s to develop an Islamic approach to environmental protection. Now as EcoIslam/IFEES, it works with other faith and secular organisations to address global heating and other environmental threats.

It was founded by Fazlun Khalid. Originally from Sri Lanka, he came to Britain in the 1950s and joined the RAF. He became deeply interested in poverty and global debt, and became committed to the environmental movement.

Aims: IFEES aims to use the environmental ethics in Islamic teaching to promote conservation and sustainable development, developing both theory and practice.

What does Islam have to say?

The word 'nature' does not appear in the Qur'an, but over 200 verses talk about creation (*khalq*). IFEES acts in response to the Qur'an's words about working for the public good. This means to do what is right, forbid what is wrong, and always act with moderation:

It is He who produces gardens, both cultivated and wild, and date-palms, and crops of diverse tastes, and olives and pomegranates, similar and dissimilar. Eat of its fruit when it yields, and give its due on the day of its harvest, and do not waste. He does not love the wasteful. (Qur'an 6:141)[1]

Muslims believe everything belongs to Allah and that people have been appointed as *khalifah* – guardians or representatives.

He made you his representatives (khalifa) on Earth … in order to test you with what He has given you. (Qur'an 6:165)[2]

IFEES draws on the *Shariah* (Islamic law) and the process of *fiqh* (the study of Islamic law). Its ideas on 'Islamic environmentalism' have grown from three general principles:

- The elements that compose the natural world are common property.
- The right to benefit from natural resources is a right held in common.
- There shall be no damage or infliction of damage, bearing in mind future users.

1 Quran in English (translation by Talal Itani) CC-BY-ND
2 Based on The Majestic Quran (translation by Musharraf Hussain) used by permission

Case study projects

IFEES/EcoIslam has applied Islamic ethical principles to develop practical projects, such as:

Green Mosques

A series of suggestions for greening mosques, including:

- providing a bus to take children home from the *madrassah*
- *Walk to Mosque* days: 'There is a reward for every step you take towards the mosque' (Hadith)
- recycling the water used in *wudu,* to water the landscape around the mosque
- creating a recycling hub at the mosque.

#PlasticFreeIftar

Encourages Muslims to raise the issues around plastic usage during the meal that breaks the fast during Ramadan, including thinking about:

- the issues of plastic usage and disposal
- choice of food and cooking materials for the meal (reducing meat, reusing plates)
- alternatives to plastic at the Iftar
- auditing plastic use more widely and taking the principles learnt at an EcoIftar into wider life.

Islam and biodiversity

The body of teaching from the Qur'an about nature is called *Ilm ul Khalq* (knowledge of creation). IFEES's responses to this include conserving the communities of animals, insects and landscapes on the Earth through projects including:

- planting trees in Africa and Indonesia through the Schools4trees programme
- forest management programmes in Indonesia
- training programmes on protecting the environment in Nigeria
- marine conservation in Zanzibar.

Links: www.ifees.org.uk

Case study 3: A Rocha UK

A Rocha is a Christian charity that works to protect and restore the natural world, equipping Christians to care for the environment.

Origins: A Rocha began as a charity in Portugal in 1983, run by Peter and Miranda Harris. A Rocha UK began from a local Christian conservation project in Southall, London, in 2001.

Aims: A Rocha UK says that its work comes from a fundamental belief: that looking after the world, in all the different forms that takes, is a core part of what it means to be a follower of Jesus.

It has five core commitments:

- *Christian*: 'Underlying all we do is our biblical faith in the living God, who made the world, loves it and entrusts it to the care of human society.'
- *Conservation*: research and education for conservation and restoration of the natural world.
- *Community*: through a commitment to God and creation, its members aim to develop good relationships with each other, the local community and A Rocha internationally.
- *Cross-cultural*: gaining insights and skills from people of diverse cultures.
- *Cooperation*: partnership with those who share concerns for a sustainable world.

What does Christianity have to say?

This charity bases its work on the beliefs held by many Christians that:

- God made the world and he loves it. If Christians love God they need to love the world and take care of it in their role as stewards of the Earth.
- People were created by God to look after the world, and this is an integral part of what it means to be human – not only for those interested in the environment.
- Human activity has caused many of the problems in the world, and we have a responsibility to act.
- God has a purpose for the world, and Christian people need to play their part in the renewal of God's world.

Some key texts:

The Lord God placed the man in the Garden of Eden as its gardener, to tend and care for it. *Genesis 2:15 (TLB)*

Israel, listen as the Lord accuses everyone in the land! No one is faithful or loyal or truly cares about God. Cursing, dishonesty, murder, robbery, unfaithfulness – these happen all the time. Violence is everywhere. And so your land is a desert. Every living creature is dying – people and wild animals, birds and fish. *Hosea 4:1–3 (CEV)*

A UK ROCHA
Caring for God's Earth

Case study projects

A Rocha UK wants to equip Christians to project and restore the environment, for God, nature and all people. Here are some of the ways they do this:

Eco Church

An audit and award scheme supporting churches to express their care for God's world in:

- how they worship
- what they teach
- how they look after their buildings and land
- the lifestyles of their members.

Wild Christian

A community of people who are supported to explore the connection between their beliefs and the environment. This scheme encourages Christians to take practical actions to nurture and protect nature while living more sustainably.

Partners in action

A Rocha supports a community of land managers across the country to conserve the land and demonstrate active care for the natural world. They participate in joint conservation work as well as supporting one another in prayer.

Links: **arocha.org.uk**

Case study 4: EcoSikh UK

EcoSikh UK is an interfaith charity set up to help combat climate change, global heating and biodiversity loss.

Origins: EcoSikh began in the Punjab and the USA in 2009, arising from the United Nations Development Programme. It spread to the UK soon after, saying that it began humbly but with a global environmental vision. It sets out to empower people to make a difference where they are.

Aims: EcoSikh UK:

- connects Sikh values, beliefs and institutions to the most important environmental issues facing our world
- draws on the Sikh Gurus and the Khalsa to shape the behaviour and outlook of Sikhs as well as the wider world
- aims to ensure that their deep reverence for all creation remains a central part of the Sikh way of life.

What does Sikhi have to say?

'Climate change is possibly one of the most serious environmental threats facing our world today. Our first Guru, Guru Nanak Dev Ji, explained that the world we humans create around ourselves is a reflection of our own inner state.' Rick Panesar, EcoSikh UK

There are lots of stories about the gurus' love for animals, birds, trees and the wider natural world. The seventh guru, Guru Har Rai, particularly taught Sikhs the importance of caring for the natural world. Many Sikhs are vegetarian, and all food that is served in the langar of the gurdwara is vegetarian. The concept of *daya* (compassion) is important to Sikh people.

Sikhs believe Waheguru has created a world which looks after all of our needs. The Earth being called our mother shows Sikhs that they need to show great respect towards the environment.

Some key texts:

'Air is our Guru, water is our father, the earth is our mother. They give us life, we sleep in their laps night and day, in which the entire world plays.' Guru Nanak in Guru Granth Sahib, p. 8.

'The God-conscious person is animated with an intense desire to do good in this world.' Guru Granth Sahib, p. 273.

Case study projects

World Sikh Environment Day

An environmental celebration day, started in the USA in 2010 and held in March every year. It is celebrated as a tribute to Guru Har Rai Ji, the seventh guru, known for his sensitivity to nature and the protection of the environment. Participants are encouraged to:

- spend time in nature
- clean up the local area, plant trees, stop driving, reduce single-use plastic
- educate themselves about protecting the environment
- find out more about Guru Har Rai Ji
- distribute *Boota Prashad*, a selection of things to allow trees or flowering plants to be planted as a reminder of the guru and to protect the environment.

Guru Nanak Sacred Forests and Guru Nanak Bagh

A series of micro-forests is being planted in India, reviving natural forest species in the region. Already over 100 native, rare and endangered species have been conserved.

This project works closely with scientists, creating a seed bank. The EcoSikh website forest section shares details such as the amount of carbon captured.

A related project is situated at a gurdwara in the Punjab where all the trees and plants referred to in the Guru Granth Sahib will be planted. The related quotes from the gurus will be displayed alongside the plants. This centre will then be used for education.

Links:

ecosikh.org
ecosikhuk.org

3 GREEN VOICES: religious and non-religious perspectives

These activities mix materials from the disciplines of religious studies, environmental science and theology to enable 11–14-year-olds in RE to think carefully about current issues of climate change, global heating and related questions of justice. Select and adapt these as appropriate to your students' prior knowledge.

A Initial reflections

Give students the questions from Resource 3.1 (p. 9). Give them time to draft some quick responses in note form. Allow them to discuss those answers with two or three classmates, then add more notes to their responses, arising from their discussions.

B Expectations: what do religions have to say?

Resource 3.2 (online) includes a selection of teachings from diverse religious traditions about how humans should treat each other. Ask students to read these and list some of the implications for climate justice, by completing this sentence starter for each: *If traditions teach this, then adherents should …* Talk about how love and care for fellow humans might (ideally) relate to love and care for the world and environment, adding notes to their questions from Activity A.

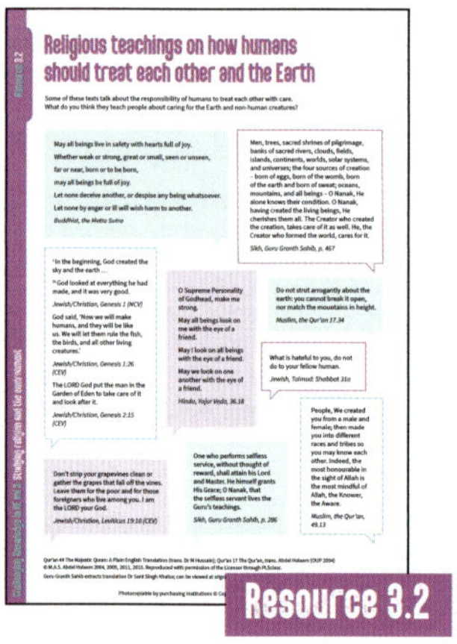

C Common concerns: listening to diverse voices

Resource 3.3 (online) offers eight articles about the environment from religious and non-religious perspectives: Jewish, Muslim, Pagan, Sikh, Christian, ethical vegan, Buddhist and Humanist. They have all been given the same questions as your students. Working in groups, give each group two articles – perhaps one from a traditional religion and one from a secular worldview. Ask students to highlight and note answers to the following:

- What are the interviewees' fears and hopes?
- Identify a core idea or teaching that is important (e.g. *tikkun olam*, *taqwa*, *daya*, ecocentric, stardust, anthropogenic, spiritual energy), and explain it.
- What specific actions do the interviewees carry out in response to environmental challenges?
- What inspires or motivates them to do this?
- Draft at least two questions they would like to ask each interviewee.

Ask each group to select two interesting or challenging ideas they encountered and report back to the class, so that all students hear from a range of perspectives.

Ask students to return to their own answers (from Activity A above), add to or amend them in the light of what they have just studied.

Resource 3.4 (pp. 10–11) offers a kind of Pinterest page, '**REinterest**'! Use this to review, summarise and clarify the relevant information, and to provoke students to a response: how do they feel about the issues around climate justice?

D Responding: rant, argue, preach or prophesy?

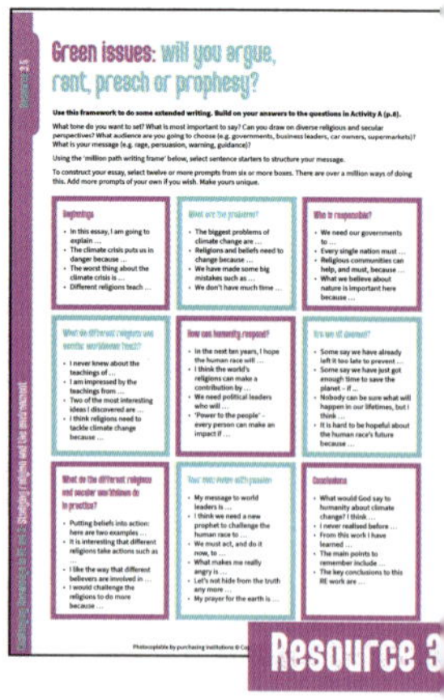

Use Resource 3.5 (online) to set up students' extended writing. Building on their answers in Activity A, amplified through the subsequent study of diverse voices, students now decide what tone they want to set. What do they think is most important to say? Can they draw on diverse religious and non-religious perspectives? What audience will they choose? (e.g. governments, business leaders, car owners, supermarkets). What is their message? (e.g. rage, persuasion, warning, guidance). Then, using Resource 3.5 (online), they select sentence starters to structure their message. When these have been written, perhaps the students could perform them to the class: are they stirred to action?

What do you think about green issues?

This set of questions allows you to think through matters of belief, practice and ethics around green issues. Draft some initial ideas and responses, then discuss with other students.

In Resource 3.3 online there is a set of interviews, with eight people from different worldviews – religious and non-religious – answering the same set. Read their responses and add to your own answers to any of the ideas that make you think. What perspectives do you share? What can you learn from this dialogue with these different worldviews?

In your own life, within your own religious or non-religious worldview, how do you see the Earth and the world of nature? Why do you value nature?	**Are we one with nature? Some people see the Earth as a spiritual entity of some kind. Explain your views about this.**
Describe a time when your awareness of green issues was enhanced or challenged.	**Scriptures and sources of wisdom speak a lot about our relation to the natural world. Choose and explain a wise saying that matters to you.**
The Earth is facing problems rooted in past exploitative attitudes to the planet. What does your religious or non-religious worldview offer to help correct these problems?	**When you consider the current environmental crisis, what gives you the hope or the courage to take action?**
What and who are your favourite examples of teaching or inspiring people from your religious or non-religious worldview that can help save the planet, and why?	**Anything else on this theme you would like to add?**

REinterest

Identifying and responding to the climate emergency

Turtles and tortoises: goodbye

Currently, half the world's tortoises and turtles are threatened with extinction. Climate change means their habitats are becoming much scarcer. It's just one example of how climate change threatens biodiversity.

Time is running out

Scientific predictions say that current levels of carbon emission will lead to over 1.5 degrees of global heating by 2030. That would be bad, and higher would be worse. We only have a few years to change global heating radically.

Greta Thunberg: famous face of climate rage

Greta, born in 2003, began school strikes against climate change, and is a leading campaigner. She rebuked leaders at the United Nations: 'We are in the beginning of a mass extinction, and all you can talk about is money and fairy tales of eternal economic growth. How *dare* you!'

Melting ice, rising sea levels

Ice sheets in Greenland and Antarctica are melting increasingly quickly – ice loss happened four times faster in 2020 than in 2003. It contributes 20 per cent of the current sea-level rise. When sea levels rise, low-lying land, from Miami to Norfolk to the Solomon Islands, is in danger of being lost to the sea.

Pope Francis

The Pope teaches that we are made from the Earth and that the fruit of the Earth sustains our life. He says humans bear the 'breath of life' that comes from God, and that we live in this common home as one family in biodiversity with God's other creatures.

So, in imitation of God's love, all people are called to care for and respect all creatures, and to offer love and compassion to their neighbours, especially the most vulnerable.

40 kg of plastic and one dead whale

A young male whale about 15 feet long had swallowed huge amounts of plastic human waste in the ocean, and starved to death. UNESCO estimates that 100,000 marine mammals die because of plastic pollution each year.

David Attenborough: Humanist prophet

The famous wildlife film maker has been talking about the impact of climate change on our world for 20 years, but things have got worse faster than he forecast to begin with. Evidence shows that dramatic action is needed in the next ten years. He says that we are running out of time but insists that there is still hope.

Play the perfect game

Bill McKibben, leading USA climate justice campaigner, says that if we are to save the planet, the whole world, every country, needs to 'play the perfect game' for the next decade.

Images: Daniele COSSU / Shutterstock.com; Danting Zhu on Unsplash; Markus Spiske on Unsplash; D'Bone Collector Museum (with thanks to Darrell Blatchley)

Matthew Neville: Christian

'Creation is presented as being something that exists in harmony with God but separate from God. Humanity is given an important role, both as part of creation and in caring for the rest of creation. A crucial difference from some forms of modern economic thinking is that the earth does not belong to humanity – we are asked to look after it, but it is not ours to do with as we please.'

Ishpal Kaur Dillon: Sikh

'The fact that the Lord is omnipresent and omnipotent is what makes the Earth and Nature a spiritual entity. In the sacred scriptures, Japji Sahib paath, Guru Nanak Dev Ji proclaims that there are countless worlds, and ours is just one of many. We are not the centre of the universe. Having a human form is the highest form of reincarnation, providing a blessed opportunity.'

Gen Kelsang Pagpa: Buddhist

'We're up against our negative minds, or "delusions", as we call them in Buddhism. These include greed, attachment and ignorance, which powerfully influence our actions. In Buddhism, we don't see the Earth as a spiritual entity, but we do need to respect it as it's our life support system – and, as is commonly said, there's no Planet B.'

James Dart: Humanist

'I believe that humans have an enormous responsibility to preserve balance and diversity in nature and … maintain a sustainable environment so that future generations may enjoy its beauty, as we have done. Whilst I subscribe to no supernatural reading of our place in the cosmos, it is undeniable that we are linked to it, and to nature, in awe-inspiring ways.'

Maegan Davies-John: ethical vegan

'The Earth and all life upon it are precious. Human beings, in my philosophy, are no more worthy of life and pleasure than any other animal, and thus no creature should be exploited for our gain. The same goes for the land and resources of the Earth; we should live consciously to reduce damage to our environment, and consume within our means.'

Belinda Twiggs: Pagan

'My philosophy or worldview sees the Earth as a living mechanism, complex, fascinating and beautiful, worthy of honour and respect. Humans are capable of great art and endeavour, always wondering and asking questions. The problem is when the lens is *ego-centric* rather than *eco-centric*; it is all about humans but it should be about the web of life.'

Nina Leigh: Jewish

'There is no question for me that we are responsible for the world that G-d created, and we must help preserve it as much as we can before it is too late. In Judaism we often use the phrase '*Tikkun Olam*', which means 'repairing the world'. Different Jewish denominations have various explanations for this, such as working towards peace and social justice, and helping the poor, but in this century more than ever we use it to literally mean 'repair the world'.'

Shaziah Gleadall: Muslim

'Islam doesn't teach that we are "one" with nature, but rather that nature is a sign of God's power. Islam focuses on the idea of humans being given the responsibility to look after the planet. Muslims are '*Khalifah*', meaning we are Allah's vice-regents and should be looking after the planet which God has provided for us. Therefore, it is a religious duty for Muslims to care for the world and think about the environmental impact of all that we do.'

What are you going to do about it?

Do you agree that everyone needs to play their part? Would you …

- *campaign for climate justice?*
- *educate yourself more about climate justice issues?*
- *use the power of religion to help people make changes in lifestyle and politics?*
- *support charities working against climate change?*
- *change your own use of petrol, meat, plastic, air travel and other unhelpful activities?*

If not … why not?

4 THINKING theologically about creation

The following sections – chapters 5–7 – explore the relationship between humans and the environment using the discipline of theology. This brings God into the equation, as theology generally starts out on the basis that there is a God. This does not mean that to do theology you must believe in God; you might say: 'Okay, assuming for the moment that God does exist, what impact does that have on people's thinking on the environment, for example?'

A What is theology and what do theologians do?

Use the Theology Investigator File (online) to explore the discipline further. For example, you might:

- give students the questions first, and ask them what they think the theologian will answer.
- give students the file questions and answers separately, for them to match up, as a way to get them to read closely.

Note the kinds of questions theology asks, the tools and methods it uses. The next few pages will explore a few questions and apply some methods.

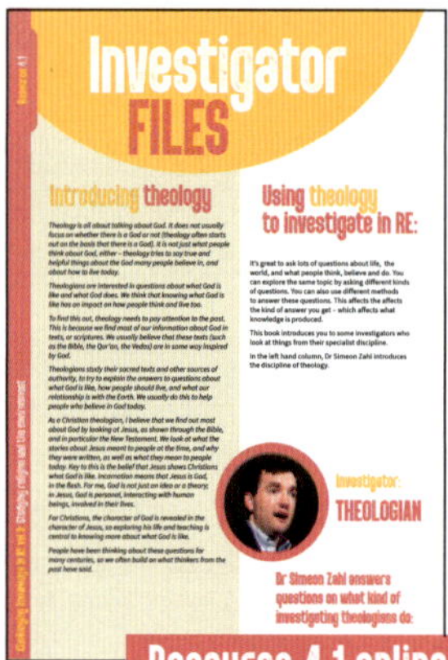

Resource 4.1 online

B Dominion and stewardship

Chapter 5 explores ideas of Christianity and creation through the concepts of dominion and stewardship (see pp. 14–15 and Resource 5.1 online). It focuses on Genesis 1:26–28 and applies the methods of theology in: analysing the text, thinking through their meaning in context, and comparing how people have interpreted it in different times. Explore with your students the implications of a shift from dominion as domination (Lynn White's accusation; see p. 14) to dominion as stewardship. You could also add relevant extracts from Genesis 2 (e.g. 2:15, 19–20)

INTERPRETING GENESIS

Chapter 6 gives students a chance to analyse the text in more detail, to try to understand what the writer(s) meant when they wrote it down. The text is available online (Resources 6.1 and 6.2 online). This version from Mary Phil Korsak is very close to the Hebrew text in its layout, its language and repetition, and its names for God. (Note the word for 'man' here is 'groundling'; it reflects the word for 'ground' = *adama*.)

Resource 6.1 online

Resource 6.2 online

C Diving into Genesis

- Revisit the creation stories in Genesis (see Resources 6.1 and 6.2 online). Working in groups, half the class study Genesis 1, the other half study Genesis 2.
- For their chapter, students could:
  - choose a piece of music to convey the tone of the chapter, and explain their choice
  - find an artwork that they think best illustrates their chapter.
- Genesis 1's God is called *Elohim*, God; Genesis 2's is called *YHWH* or *Yahweh Elohim*, LORD God in most translations. Ask students to look for evidence about what God is like in their chapter.

- Discuss what differences they have found between the chapters, and talk about the nature of God as presented in Genesis 1 and 2. Are these conflicting or coherent? (To help with this, see p. 16, the introduction to Christian readings of Genesis.)
- Ask students to think about the relationship between God and the natural world, between humans and God, and between humans and the natural world, as presented in the chapters. Get them to summarise these views.

D Genesis through the ages: thinking things through

Pages 18–19 give a selection of key theologians commenting on ideas of creation, humanity and the environment in Genesis (note extended texts are available online, Resource 6.5). Resource 6.3 (p. 17) offers a way into these more demanding texts, with a selection of the key theological ideas. Some activity ideas are on that page.

Extended extracts from Genesis

Resource 6.5 online

Select from the following ideas, as appropriate to your students and context:

- Ask students to highlight any connections they can make to the two Genesis chapters they have been studying.
- Give students pp. 18–19. Ask them to match the key ideas on p. 17 with the longer texts.
- Ask them to choose two texts from pp. 18–19 – one ancient and one more recent. Note the contexts: look at the date and place of writing (if known). Identify at least two clues in the writing that reflect the context. Read each text carefully. Underline, look up and define any unfamiliar words. Highlight in different colours the words that focus on God, the Earth and human beings.
- Get them to use the longer extracts to elaborate the key ideas from p. 17 with an additional sentence or two. What questions do the texts raise for them?
- As a class, analyse the texts together. List the ways in which the texts:
    - show what God is like
    - show what it means for humans to be 'in the image of God'
    - have implications for the relationship between humans and the natural world.
- Theologians are interested in how past traditions interpreted texts. As a class, can you discern any changes in perspective through the ages here? Are some ideas held throughout? Do changing circumstances have an impact on theological responses?
- Building on the dominion/stewardship work in chapter 5, ask students to create a flow chart to show whether/how views on these two ideas changed. (Note how Calvin in the sixteenth century was talking about stewardship. What was the change that led to Lynn White's critique (see p. 14)?)

E Evaluating ideas

- Refer to the Theology Investigator File (online). Apply the tools of theology to evaluate how far Christian teachings on the environment are:
- **coherent** (do they make sense overall?)
- **faithful** (do they reflect the wider Christian tradition?)
- **fruitful** (do they help Christians to flourish?)
- **significant** (to what extent do these Christian principles have significance for people outside the Christian tradition?)
- Ask students to reflect on what is similar and different between this Christian worldview and their own. You could encourage a creative response: a collage, a poem, a photomontage, perhaps?

F Islamic perspectives

Chapter 7 (pp. 20–21) gives students an opportunity to learn about an Islamic perspective. Start by giving them a careful reading of Professor Lejla Demiri's introduction – highlighting and defining challenging words – and asking them to draw lines between the introduction and any of the relevant selected texts. Resource 7.1 (p. 21) encourages some deeper thinking and reflection. Examine the connections between dominion, stewardship and *khalifah* – variously translated as guardian, trustee, vicegerent (deputy), successor.

7 Creation and the environment: an Islamic perspective

God and the sustainability of the earth: interpreting Islamic traditions

pp. 20–21

Note: the Green Muslims website offers extensive Quranic extracts on green issues: **www.greenmuslims.org/green-scriptures**

5 Christianity and creation: the language of dominion and stewardship

In Christianity there are many different views about the ideas of dominion and stewardship. These pages contain just some of them. Before you go any further, check you know the meaning of the words dominion and stewardship. In the context of Christianity, these words are often linked to ideas about the Earth, how it has been treated in the past, and how humans should behave towards it.

What is the relationship between humans and creation?

26 Then God said, 'Let Us make man in Our image, according to Our likeness; let them have dominion over the fish of the sea, over the birds of the air, and over the cattle, over all the earth and over every creeping thing that creeps on the earth.'

27 So God created man in His own image; in the image of God He created him; male and female He created them.

28 Then God blessed them, and God said to them, 'Be fruitful and multiply; fill the earth and subdue it; have dominion over the fish of the sea, over the birds of the air, and over every living thing that moves on the earth.'

Genesis 1:26–28 (NKJV)

Many parts of the Bible talk about the relationship between humans and the environment, but the passage above is often credited as having allowed humans to treat the environment badly.

Find the parts of Genesis 1:26–28 which:

i. show humans to be made in the image of God
ii. suggest that humans should have power over the Earth and all creatures.

Why might these ideas cause people to treat the environment in harmful ways?

Has Christianity caused harm?

In his 1967 article entitled 'The Historical Roots of Our Ecologic Crisis', *Science* 155, the historian Lynn White Jr argues that Christian thinking where *dominion* has come to mean *dominate* or *exploit* has led people to damage the environment. White says:

- Christianity is the most anthropocentric (human-centred) religion.
- In the past, humans associated rivers, trees, the sun and so on, with Gods and spirits, and so naturally treated them with respect.
- By seeing God as Creator of all of nature and not part of it, many Christians have interpreted the Bible as seeing humans (who the Bible says are made in God's image) as having power over all creation.
- In Western interpretations of Genesis 2, man's naming of the animals asserts his dominance over them.
- Western Christians have interpreted this to mean that all of creation was planned for humanity's benefit and rule.

White does not argue that religion should be rejected, but rather that Christianity should be re-thought, or a new religion found to help the world out of the ecologic crisis.

Not everyone agrees with White that people's exploitation of nature has been caused by Christian thinking. Many interpret the passage from Genesis as instructing Christians to look after the Earth with care, as a gardener or caretaker: *dominion* becomes *stewardship.*

What if the end of the world is coming?

Not all Christians today believe environmental issues to be important considerations. One reason given by some of those Christians is to do with future, eschatological (end of the world) events.

For example, some Christians take texts such as 2 Peter 3:10–15 literally, and seriously. This text talks of the heavens and Earth being destroyed in fire and looks forward to a new heaven and Earth to come, where righteousness dwells. Christians who believe that the Earth is not going to last for ever may respond differently – especially if they think the end of the world is close at hand:

- Some say it is more important to focus on being righteous and helping others to understand how to be good Christians than to spend time worrying about the environment.

- Some Christians are not worried about exploiting the Earth – they say it's okay to do it, as there will be a new Earth in the future.

However, the Bible presents different views on what will happen in the future. Some Christians believe that rather than the destruction of this world there will be a transformation, so caring for it now can help to transform it for the better.

Care for the environment in Christianity

Many Christians see caring for the environment as essential. Numerous Christian organisations and charities have been set up for this reason.

Pope Francis has been outspoken about the importance of the environment for Christians. In 2015 he wrote a letter to the Catholic Church on this topic, called *Laudato si'* ('Praise Be'). In it, Pope Francis explains that:

- Humans should have close relationships with God, the rest of humankind and the Earth.
- However, these relationships have been broken due to sin.
- Humankind has not recognised the limitations of its being creatures rather than being God.
- The command to 'have dominion' over the Earth from Genesis 1:28 has become distorted to the extent that humans are in conflict with the planet rather than living in harmony with it.
- Saint Francis is held up as an example, as he lived harmoniously with creatures.

Pope Francis acknowledges that Christians have interpreted the Bible incorrectly in the past. He says that Christians must not support the idea that humans can have complete domination over other creatures because they are created in God's image and have been given dominion over the Earth. Dominion should *not* be seen as domination; it should be viewed as 'responsible stewardship'.

Stewardship

The idea of stewardship is widespread in modern Christianity, but not all Christians support it:

- Some are concerned that the word 'stewardship' focuses too much on humans as carers for God's creation, so would prefer a less human-centred word – one that gives equality to non-human creatures.
- Others believe that it is biblically incorrect to talk about humans as stewards, because the Bible talks of dominion, not stewardship.

Teaching and learning

Many people try to reconcile their beliefs with the practicalities of life. For example, some people:

- try to care for the environment and non-human creatures by becoming vegan
- continue to eat meat but try to ensure that no part of an animal is wasted, and it is all eaten
- would like to eat in non-wasteful ways, but financial issues mean they have to buy whichever meat is on offer at the supermarket.

Apply your learning about dominion and stewardship to three scenarios. Take four characters:

- a Christian who is concerned about the environment
- a Christian who is not concerned about the environment
- a character of your choosing
- yourself.

In pairs or small groups, read through the scenarios. For each, place all four characters where you think they would stand on a continuum line from *totally agree* to *totally disagree*, giving thoughtful reasons for your placements.

Scenario 1: 'My friend says that if an animal is slaughtered for meat, we should make sure we use all parts of the animal, so nothing is wasted. This is responsible stewardship, and being wasteful with dead animals is not. So we should all be wearing a lot more fur and leather, because animal fur and skin are not worthless parts of a creature. Do you agree with this idea?'

Scenario 2: 'Our next-door neighbours are really environmentally friendly. They try to reuse rather than throw things away or recycle, always care for the local wildlife in our street, and join in with local environmental causes (such as litter picks). I asked if they would like to help me raise money to save the rainforest, but they explained that although they care for the environment, there's so much for them to do that they have decided to spend their time on local issues, not national or international. Is it ethical to prioritise in this way?'

Scenario 3: 'My family has always taught me that the end of the world is very close. The Bible mentions many signs of this, such as famine, plague and war. We spend tons of effort trying to help people understand about Jesus and be righteous Christians so that they too can gain eternal life when the time comes. But my schoolmates and teachers seem to think the world is unlikely to end soon, so we should help make the planet an amazing place for future generations. Should I follow their lead?'

See Resource 5.1 online for definitions, and additional teaching and learning ideas.

6 How have Christians interpreted Genesis through the ages?

Overview

As Christians have faced different circumstances through the ages, their attitudes to creation have changed. Theologies and biblical interpretations have changed too, as the text itself faces up to the ever-changing contemporary context.

Early interpreters of Genesis did not seem to worry about whether God had or had not created the Earth – it was generally taken as true. They did not really see any contradictions between Genesis 1 and 2 either – chapter 2 seems to zoom in on Day 6 from chapter 1. However, discussion did consider questions such as whether creation was instantaneous. If so, it would mean that the seven days in Genesis 1 were allegorical rather than referring to the literal passage of time, and that the events described point to spiritual truths. Thus an influential interpreter like Augustine interpreted the creation of light on Day 1 as being about the light of wisdom by which creatures can come to know God rather than the sort of light we see with our eyes.

It was in the late nineteenth century that biblical studies identified the different sources behind the opening chapters of Genesis. Chapter 1 uses the word *Elohim* for God, whereas chapter 2 uses the word YHWH (usually transcribed now as Yahweh). This led many to focus on the idea that these were two distinctly different accounts. Some say they were contradictory, but others see them as presenting two ways of viewing the Creator. In the latter view, Genesis 1 emphasises the transcendent nature of God, creating the universe by speaking it into being, while Genesis 2 focuses on God's caring and intimate relationship with his creation – up close and personal with humans in the garden.

As people have become more aware of the damage that humans have done to the environment, especially since the industrial revolution in the eighteenth century, some have looked again at the language of dominion or rule in Genesis 1:28. One of these was Lynn White Jr, writing in 1967. He suggested that Christians had interpreted '*dominion*' as meaning 'domination', and this resulted in Christians believing the Earth existed only for their benefit, so that they could ransack it for whatever they needed. This interpretation was often connected to the discussion of the 'image of God' in Genesis 1:26–27, which was read by some as indicating that the needs of humans are more important than those of other creatures.

At the same time, many Christians have pointed back to the description in Genesis 2:15, where the human being is 'to work and care for' the garden, emphasising the idea of *stewardship*, saying that this is what 'dominion' really means. The idea that God intended humans to be custodians rather than overlords of creation is not new (see Philo, Resource 6.4), but it has become more widespread in the modern era due to the growing sense of environmental crisis.

Key ideas about creation from theology

Below are nine ideas about the relationship between humans, the Creator and the creation. They reflect the views of theologians from the first to the twenty-first centuries.

a. *Read the statements and make any connections you can between any of them.*
b. *Are there any clues as to which ones are ancient and which are modern?*
c. *Connect these statements with biblical texts from Genesis 1 and 2. Do these statements focus on particular ideas of God and human beings?*
d. *List at least three kinds of behaviour you would expect to arise as a result of the ideas summed up in the statements: how do they suggest humans should treat the natural world?*
e. *Match the statements to the quotations from theologians on pp. 18–19. Using at least two texts, add another sentence to the relevant summaries below.*
f. *These theologians take it for granted that there is a God. In a secular society, what helpful insights might they offer to non-religious people about human relationships with nature?*

God's care of creation is ongoing and sustaining. God looks after creation, just as a father looks after his children, or an artist cares for his art. He won't let it be harmed.

Philo

It is our mind – our ability to reason – that separates us from animals. This is what it means to be made in the image of God. And this is why God gave humans 'dominion'.

Augustine

Humans are given the earth to care for and use, to pass on to future generations in as good or better condition. They should not abuse it through greed or carelessness.

Calvin

Genesis creation narratives reveal profound truths about the relationship between:

- humans and God
- humans and each other
- humans and the Earth.

They show that all three relationships have been broken through sin.

Pope Francis

Genesis creation stories are anthropocentric – humans are at the centre, being made in the image of God. But this is part of God's loving act of creation, not for evil. Some Christians see humans as being a bit like hamsters in God's hamster cage. Everything in the cage is for our benefit. Others say it is more that humans are servants of God – privileged to care for the Earth on behalf of the Creator.

Janet Martin Soskice

There is little point in arguing about the order of the days in Genesis. Instead, people should consider that Genesis 1 shows just how good and generous God is towards humans: everything is in place before humans are created.

Luther

It is essential to interpret the 'dominion' texts in the light of Adam's loving relationship with the environment, and the wider biblical call to care for the land, for domestic and wild animals.

John Chryssavgis

The Earth is God's – humans cannot claim ownership. We cannot justify domination over other creatures. We are in a mutual relationship of responsibility for humans and nature.

Pope Francis

With the power of being ruler of creation comes great responsibility: disobedience can (will) lead to judgment and loss.

Ellen Davis

Making sense of creation in Genesis: texts through the ages

Christians have interpreted the Genesis creation narratives in different ways through the ages. Dr Simeon Zahl has selected some examples from Christian theologians. They have been selected to show how different connections have been made between the biblical text and human behaviour. On p. 13 there are some ideas for exploring these texts. Resource 6.5 (online) gives extended texts.

Philo was a Jewish thinker who lived in Alexandria, Egypt, around the time of Jesus. He brought together Hebrew and Greek ideas. Some say his writing influenced the apostle Paul. Here he writes about God's ongoing provision and care for creation:

It stands to reason that what has been brought into existence should be cared for by its Father and Maker. For, as we know, it is a father's aim in regard of his offspring and [a craftsman's] in regard of his handiwork to preserve them, and by every means to fend off from them [anything] that may entail loss or harm. He keenly desires to provide for them in every way all that is beneficial and to their advantage[.]

Philo of Alexandria (c.20 BCE-40 CE) *On the Account of the World's Creation Given by Moses*
trans. F.H. Colson and G.H. Whitaker, Loeb Classical Library (Harvard University Press, 1981). First published 1929. Loeb Classical Library ® is a registered trademark of the President and Fellows of Harvard College. All rights reserved.

Augustine was born in Hippo (in modern-day Algeria) in the fourth century, and later became bishop there. He is one of the most influential Christian thinkers. Here he considers what it means to be made 'in the image of God':

We are quite right … to take the words, 'Let us make man to our image and likeness' (Genesis 1:26) as referring to … the innermost and principal element in humanity … the mind. It is from this element, after all, … which separates it from that of the brute beasts, that the worth of the whole human being is to be reckoned. The other things in us, though beautiful in their kind, are still common to us and animals, and therefore in us are to be priced cheaply.

Augustine (354–430 CE) *Unfinished Literal Commentary on Genesis* (c. 415)
trans. Edmund Hill (New York, New City Press, 2002)

Martin Luther was a German monk, pastor and theologian. He began the Protestant Reformation with his criticisms of the Roman Catholic Church. Commenting here on Genesis 1:11, he rejects the literal speculations raised by some people about the order of days. Instead, he says:

I prefer that we reflect on the divine solicitude [i.e. care] and benevolence toward us, because He provided such an attractive dwelling place for the future human being before the human being was created. Thus … when man is created, he finds a ready and equipped home into which he is brought by God and commanded to enjoy all the riches of so splendid a home. On the third day He provides [storeroom] and provisions. On the fourth, sun and moon are given to man for attendance and service. On the fifth the rule over the fish and the birds is turned over to him. On the sixth the rule over all the beasts is turned over to him, so that he might enjoy all this wealth free, in proportion to his need. And all this generosity is intended to make man recognize the goodness of God and live in the fear of God.

Martin Luther (1483–1546) *Lectures on Genesis* (c. 1535)
trans. George V. Schick
From Luther's Works 1 © 1953, 1986 Concordia Publishing House www.cph.org

John Calvin, one of the foremost theologians of the Protestant Reformation, was a pastor in Geneva, Switzerland in the sixteenth century. He wrote a commentary on Genesis 2:15:

The custody of the garden was given in charge to Adam, to show that we possess the things which God has committed to our hands, on the condition, that being content with the frugal and moderate use of them, we should take care of what shall remain. Let him who possesses a field, so partake of its yearly fruits, that he may not suffer the ground to be injured by his negligence; but let him endeavour to hand it down to posterity as he received it, or even better cultivated. Let him so feed on its fruits, that he neither dissipates it by luxury, nor permits [it] to be marred or ruined by neglect. Moreover, that this economy, and this diligence, with respect to those good things which God has given us to enjoy, may flourish among us, let everyone regard himself as the steward of God in all things which he possesses. Then he will neither conduct himself dissolutely, nor corrupt by abuse those things which God requires to be preserved.

John Calvin (1509–1564) *Commentary on Genesis* (c.1550)
Christian Classics Ethereal Library

In his 2015 circular letter to the Church, *Laudato si': On Care for our Common Home*, Pope Francis addresses the need to take global action to address the environmental crisis. In sections 66–68, he refers to ways in which Genesis has been interpreted incorrectly:

66. The creation accounts in the book of Genesis … suggest that human life is grounded in three fundamental and closely intertwined relationships: with God, with our neighbour and with the earth itself. According to the Bible, these three vital relationships have been broken, both outwardly and within us. This rupture is sin. The harmony between the Creator, humanity and creation as a whole was disrupted by our presuming to take the place of God and refusing to acknowledge our creaturely limitations. This in turn distorted our mandate to 'have dominion' over the earth (cf. *Gen* 1:28), to 'till it and keep it' (*Gen* 2:15). …

67. … [N]owadays we must forcefully reject the notion that our being created in God's image and given dominion over the earth justifies absolute domination over other creatures. The biblical texts are to be read in their context, with an appropriate hermeneutic [theory of interpretation], recognising that they tell us to 'till and keep' the garden of the world (cf. *Gen* 2:15). 'Tilling' refers to cultivating, ploughing or working, while 'keeping' means caring, protecting, overseeing and preserving. This implies a relationship of mutual responsibility between human beings and nature. …

68. This responsibility for God's earth means that human beings, endowed with intelligence, must respect the laws of nature and the delicate equilibria existing between the creatures of this world … Clearly, the Bible has no place for a tyrannical anthropocentrism unconcerned for other creatures.

Pope Francis (born 1936)
Laudato si', 2015

John Chryssavgis is a Greek Orthodox theologian from Australia. He is the theological advisor on environmental issues to the Ecumenical Patriarch. Here, Chryssavgis argues that how people treat the environment reflects their relationship with God.

For centuries [Genesis 1:28] … has provided the licence to dominate and abuse the world according to our selfish needs and purposes. … The Genesis passage should instead be understood in the context of Adam's naming of the animals … This event itself implies a loving and lasting personal relationship on the part of Adam with the environment ... The 'dominion' texts denoting the 'power' of humanity over the world must in fact always be interpreted in light of human responsibility toward nature, whereby one is called to care for the land (Lev. 25:1–5), for domesticated animals (Deut. 25:4), and even for wildlife (Deut. 22:6). We fall short of our vocation when we fail to care for creation. In fact, by refusing that call, we cause the world to remain a wasteland, unable to come alive by the compassion of a vital human being, who becomes the conscience, eyes, voice, and ears of the earth.

John Chryssavgis (b. 1958), 'The Earth as Sacrament' *The Oxford Handbook of Religion and Ecology* 2006, ed. Roger S Gottlieb

Ellen Davis teaches Old Testament theology at Duke University in North Carolina, USA. She is particularly interested in how the land and the environment are portrayed in the Bible. Here, she underlines the great risks and responsibilities involved in being stewards of God's creation:

What is *stated* in Genesis 1:28 is that humans play a special role, both powerful and responsible, in maintenance of the order that God has established. The earth may be 'conquered', that is, claimed for God's purposes and rendered hospitable to the whole created order. Opposition to God, from whatever quarter, can be overcome. What is left *unstated* here – but should be burned into the memory and moral understanding of those who hear – is that land, the habitable earth, can be lost in penalty for disobedience. Again, what is left unsaid, but is clarified in the third chapter of Genesis and then reinforced time and again through the rest of Scripture, is that humans are the primary source of opposition to God, the source of most if not all threats to the integrity of the created order … [H]earers … [aware] of exile must at least suspect the presence of a silent judgment.

Ellen Davis (b. 1950), *Scripture, Culture, and Agriculture* (CUP 2012)

Janet Martin Soskice is a Canadian-English theologian and philosopher. A Roman Catholic, for many years she was a professor at Cambridge University. Here she explores two metaphors for understanding the idea that creation is anthropocentric (human-centred):

Human beings have a privileged role to play in God's creative love because, according to [the Genesis story], they are made in the image of God. This is anthropocentric, but not necessarily malevolently so. One can distinguish two versions of Christian anthropocentrism, both of which have their advocates. In what we might call 'divine hamster cage' anthropocentrism, God is the hamster-owner, and we human beings are the hamsters. God creates the world as a kind of vivarium for human beings. The rest of the created order is our lettuce leaves and clean sawdust, completely at our disposal … In what we might call 'divine servant' or 'divine regent' anthropocentrism, on the other hand, human beings are integrally part of the whole of the created order, but they have a privileged responsibility within it; rights are attended by responsibility. Women and men are made 'in the image of God' not to ravage God's creation but to attend to it, both by caring for it and by praising it.

Janet Martin Soskice (b. 1951)
The Kindness of God (OUP 2007)

7 Creation and the environment: an Islamic perspective

Professor Lejla Demiri talks here about an Islamic perspective on the relationship between God, creation and the environment:

God created humanity from one man and one woman, says the Qur'an (see Q 49:13). This is traditionally understood to stipulate equality among people, and to teach humility. If we as human beings have the same origin, there is nothing in our humanness (colour, gender, ethnicity, etc.) that would make us superior to others.

The Prophet's instruction, 'Love for humanity what you love for yourself', further provides a principle by which one should treat others.

In another saying the Prophet uses the metaphor of 'family' to describe the bond between the Creator and His creation: 'All of creation are a family of God, and the most beloved to Him are those who are the kindest to His family.'

Creation as family refers to the fact that all things need God and depend on Him, and that human beings should care for one another as equal members of that family. This also makes it clear that our connection to God is closely defined by our relationship with other human beings as well as with non-human creation.

Human beings are 'created by God' – and they share this createdness with the entire universe, including the animal world and plants. The Qur'an addresses humanity with a clear statement that all creatures in the animal world are 'communities like yourselves' (Q 6:38).

There is a purpose in God's creation; and everything that exists glorifies the Creator by fulfilling their role in the universe, whether that is cattle producing milk or a bee making honey (Q 6:65–69).

There is a balance set by God's care, and humanity has the task of preserving this balance. 'Corruption on land and sea' should be categorically avoided, and underlines the Qur'an 30:41, a message that can be read as a firm prohibition of environmental exploitation.

Humanity is given the role of '*vicegerency' (khalifah)*, a responsibility to guard and care for creation. In sum, to gain nearness to God is made conditional upon how we behave towards our social and natural environment.

Texts

People, We created you from a male and female; then made you into different races and tribes so you may know each other. The most honourable in the sight of God is the most mindful of God, the Knower, the Aware. (Qur'an 49:13)

Remember when Your Lord told the Angels: 'I am creating a representative [*khalifah*] on Earth'. They replied: 'Are You creating someone who will make trouble there and shed blood? Is it not enough that we glorify You with praises and proclaim Your Holiness?' He said: 'I know what you don't know'. (Qur'an 2:30)

He appointed you His vice-regents [*khalifah*] on Earth. (Qur'an 35:39)

There is no creature on land or a bird flying in the sky that does not belong to a community [*ummah*] just like yours. (Qur'an 6:38)

The Seven Heavens and the Earth and what is in them all glorify Him; there isn't a single thing that doesn't glorify and praise Him, but you don't understand their way of celebrating His Glory. He is the Gentle and the Forgiving. (Qur'an 17:44)

Haven't you considered, everything in the Heavens and the Earth glorifies God? The birds flying in flocks, each one knows how it should pray and glorify Him; and God knows what they do. (Qur'an 24:41)

He raised the sky and finely balanced everything, so don't disturb the fine balance. (Qur'an 55:7–8)

Love for humanity what you love for yourself. (Hadith: Bukhārī, *Ṣaḥīḥ*)

All of creation are a family of God, and the most beloved to Him are those who are the kindest to His family. (Hadith: Bayhaqī, *Shuʿab al-īmān*)

No Muslim plants a tree or sows a seed, and then a bird, or a human, or an animal eats from it, but that it is regarded as charity from Him. (Hadith: Bukhārī, *Ṣaḥīḥ*)

Qur'an verses listed under 'Texts' are from The Majestic Qur'an: A Plain English Translation (2nd ed. 2019), trans. Dr Musharraf Hussain (Invitation Publishing). Used with permission.

God and the sustainability of the earth: interpreting Islamic traditions

In the Holy Qur'an, God is the Creator of everything, the Sustainer of life on Earth and the One who balances creation. God has made humans his *khalifah* – trustees, guardians or vicegerents – on Earth. Muslim attitudes to the creation are worked out from the verse in the Qur'an, answering the question: what does it mean to be God's trustee in caring for the world he made?

i. With a partner, read the Quranic text and the eight interpretations around it. For each one, say to your partner at least one practical difference it would make in the life of a Muslim – how would they act as a result, and why?
ii. Decide together which interpretation is most likely to have an impact on a Muslim and why. There is no single right answer – it depends on all kinds of factors – but think carefully and offer explanations.

A. All good Muslims should thank God for their lives – it's God who created us.	**B.** This verse shows clearly why Muslims, along with people of other faiths, should treat the Earth with respect – it's because God made it, so we have no right to spoil it.	**C.** It is understanding our role as guardians of the balance of the Earth established by God that leads some Muslims to campaign for ecological causes, to be eco-workers for God's world.
D. 'The Explanation' is '*al-bayan*' – speech, thought, reason; you can read it as a way of looking at human science – good Muslim scientists submit their knowledge to God, and recognise that God alone is the 'All Knowing'.	**'The All Merciful has taught the Qur'an. He [God] created man and taught him the Explanation. The sun and the moon run their measured circuits, the stars and the trees bow themselves. Heaven – He raised it up and set the Balance. Transgress not in the balance.'** Qur'an, 55:1–7	**E.** Nature is balanced by God, and by all other species – it is only humans that corrupt the world and destroy the balance. It is part of our submission to God that we keep the balance of life too.
F. In this verse, even the trees bow to God – but humans often don't; they corrupt the Earth instead. God is merciful, but will judge.	**G.** 'The Balance' that God has set may be the scales of justice that are to be used on the Day of Judgment.	**H.** God's blessings include all that is good in nature and creation. We should not disown or deny these blessings, but cherish them and rejoice in them. Good Muslims will love nature.

iii. Use Professor Demiri's explanation (p. 20) and this information to write a 75-word summary of your understanding of 'Why Muslims care about the environment'.
iv. Swap summaries with a partner – what did they get that you missed?
v. What is similar and different between this Islamic worldview and your own? What influences your worldview?

8 Investigator FILES

Using natural sciences to investigate the ENVIRONMENT

Introducing natural sciences

The natural sciences are all about describing, understanding and predicting natural processes and the world around us. They are often split into two main branches: (1) the life sciences, which you may know as biology, and (2) the physical sciences, which include physics, chemistry, geology (studying rocks) and astronomy (studying space). Whatever the branch, or area of study, all natural scientists are interested in measuring and observing nature, and placing this knowledge into theories and frameworks that help us to understand, explain and predict how the natural world works.

All natural scientists try to make sure any measurements or data that we collect can be looked at closely, and compared, by other scientists working on the same subject. This approach is referred to as the scientific method. Often this approach involves:

- *reading what other prior studies have said on the same subject*
- *posing a hypothesis—a prediction about what you think your observations are going to show*
- *designing an experiment that limits the number of variables, enables you to test your hypothesis, and allows others to copy your experiment to see if they can replicate the results*
- *analysing the data recorded, particularly in the context of previous studies done on the same subject*
- *and drawing a conclusion in relation to the original hypothesis posed.*

For many natural scientists these experiments will take place in a controlled environment, usually a laboratory similar to ones at your school. However, in some areas of the natural sciences experiments may be done outside. An example is environmental science, where scientists are interested in understanding large-scale natural processes and how humans damage them. Other experiments that environmental scientists do may be on a global scale, using data from satellites orbiting the Earth.

As the natural sciences are so wide and varied in their focus and approaches, for the rest of this investigator file we are going to focus attention on environmental science.

It's great to ask lots of questions about life, the world, and what people think, believe and do. You can explore the same topic by asking different kinds of questions. You can use different methods for answering these questions, too. This affects the kind of answer you get – which affects what knowledge is produced.

We are going to introduce you to some investigators who look at things from their specialist discipline. Here, our resident natural sciences expert, Dr Alex Hall, introduces the disciplines of natural sciences.

Investigator: ENVIRONMENTAL SCIENTIST

Dr Alex Hall outlines some key features of environmental science:

What do you investigate?

Environmental scientists measure and analyse the natural world to try and better understand how Earth's systems operate. The scientific data we collect is used to better understand how natural systems operate and how humans are affecting natural processes, and to predict how systems will change in the future. Major areas of study in environmental science include climate change, biodiversity loss, plastic contamination and air pollution.

Environmental scientists come from lots of different disciplines within the natural sciences. To answer complex questions about how human society affects the natural world, we often work with those from other disciplines such as economics and sociology.

What kinds of questions do you ask?

Environmental scientists ask questions about how natural processes occur and how they interact with each other. We are interested in all sizes of processes, from the very small to the global. So one scientist may ask why snowflakes are all different shapes. Another may be interested in whether less snow is falling across the world than used to in the past.

Increasingly, we are interested in questions which help us understand how all of the different natural systems and processes interact with each other. For example, does heavy snowfall in winter affect the amount of carbon dioxide that the land can store?

How do you find out the answers?

We go out and measure the things we are interested in. While sometimes this could be as simple as measuring the depth of a stream with a ruler, more complicated problems, like measuring the depth of an ocean, will probably require lots of scientists to collaborate, using hi-tech equipment.

Often scientists are interested in how natural processes have changed over time, so most experiments will involve repeating measurements regularly, and also trying to work out what things were like in the past.

What tools do you use?

Tools used by environmental scientists include physical objects used to help measure and quantify natural processes; they range from simple things like rulers to complex computers that can measure things like the concentration of gases in the atmosphere.

As well as these physical tools, we also use theoretical ones, such as mathematical formulas, to help us understand and explain the natural processes we have measured.

What evidence do you look for?

We often build our hypotheses off an initial observation or idea. We will then attempt to quantify or measure the process and see if our initial idea was along the right lines.

Most commonly we look for evidence that can be put into numerical form: how deep, how wide, how many? How do things change over time?

What assumptions do you need to look out for?

Once a scientist has gathered a lot of data on a problem, we may be able to spot trends. However, we need to be extra careful when analysing data and moving from describing trends to explaining the ultimate *cause* of the trend. We sometimes describe this challenge by saying that **correlation does not equal causality**. That is, although one thing may be linked to another, that does *not* mean it caused it.

What are the basic methods you use?

We use the same methods as most other scientists. Sometimes referred to as the scientific method, the process involves: **reading prior science** on the same subject; posing a **hypothesis**; designing an **experiment** to test the hypothesis; **analysing the data** collected to see if it proves or disproves the hypothesis.

How do you evaluate your methods and conclusions?

One way we evaluate our methods and conclusions is to get other scientists to read our findings. This could be **comparing our results** to other prior work on the same subject, or simply by asking other scientists to try and **copy our experiments**.

In science, if someone else can easily repeat our experiment and get the same results, we call this **repeatability** or **replicability**. This is a vital step before our data, hypothesis and new ideas can be accepted as standard scientific knowledge.

Can you apply your answers to everyone?

Most of the natural processes studied by environmental scientists can be applied to other places. For example, if one scientist uses a river in Brazil to measure how quickly sand fills the river, this information will be useful for those studying rivers elsewhere.

However, environmental scientists have to be careful about different local factors that might influence their results, especially when there is a lot of human interference in the natural system they are studying. For example, if the river in Brazil is having chemicals dumped in it by humans, then the findings from this river might not be directly comparable to other rivers around the world.

9 USING natural sciences

to explore the relationship between people and the environment

Overview

When looking at the interface between religions and science, RE has tended to look at cosmology and evolution, setting up the range of potential relationships with the Genesis creation story. This unit focuses instead on examining the extent and limitations of natural sciences, with particular reference to environmental science, and also focuses on the extent and limits of religion in debates about the environment.

Students get an opportunity to explore the questions and methods of natural sciences through the investigator file, before working through some scenarios that explore the application of science and religion to contemporary issues. These examine ideas of climate change and the idea that we now live in a new geological epoch, the Anthropocene.

Students will appreciate that scientists can gather compelling data on the situation, but that to decide what actions to take as a result of the data requires the input of other disciplines and communities. For RE, our focus will be on the contribution that religious worldviews can make to deciding what is right, good, wise and necessary. However, students will see that other communities are prominent in making decisions to take neutral data and turn it into action. Ethical, political, cultural and practical dimensions intersect. Religious worldviews will be regarded by participants with varied importance, from central to irrelevant. What they do offer, however, are systems of values people may use to weigh up decision-making: whose needs take priority and why – the Earth's, human or non-human? Individuals or communities? Rich or poor? Our world or 'God's world'? This generation or future generations?

Context

This unit fits in with the study of religious responses to the environment for examination classes. It also includes exploration of matters of climate justice that are so pertinent and vital to students (and teachers) of all ages.

Essential knowledge

Substantive knowledge includes:

- Environmental science is part of the natural sciences; it follows the scientific method to examine the natural world; it has made hugely significant contributions to our understanding of the impact of climate change on our environment, and offers evidence upon which we can base predictions.
- Religious and non-religious traditions offer guidance on how we should relate to the natural world.
- Religions may not provide specific teaching on the contemporary situation, but in general religious traditions do provide principles and values that can be applied.
- Our own worldviews – whether religious or non-religious – also affect our responses and our actions.
- It is possible to argue that a prophetic role in society (pointing out injustices and moral failures, for example) that has in the past been undertaken by religion, has been adopted or assumed by secular communities, and notably spoken through the voices of scientists and broadcasters.

Disciplinary knowledge includes:

- Environmental science, as an example of a natural science, uses diverse methods to gather data.
- There is some disagreement about what should be done once the relevant data is compiled and the trends or issues found.
- For example, the data gathered on climate change is effectively neutral: its actual and potential impact on human and non-human creatures is descriptive. However, there is debate among scientists as to just how far the science should then go to prescribe action and then demand it. Such decisions might be seen to be ethical or political, for instance.
- Theological, philosophical and ethical contributions from religious and non-religious perspectives offer guidelines for deciding on actions.

Progression

As a focus for students, here are some outcomes that relate to substantive and disciplinary knowledge, aimed at most 14-year-olds. They are based on a set of outcomes you can see on the NATRE website (link below). You will need to adapt these to suit the age and stage of your students.

Students can:

- describe the methods of environmental science and some of its findings, and offer a critical analysis of both
- analyse data from science on climate change, and apply religious and non-religious values to practical challenges
- give reasoned explanations, drawing on sources of authority, for how and why religious and non-religious traditions respond to the natural world in light of the climate crisis
- evaluate how far science and religion can go in terms of guiding human actions
- express well-informed and self-aware accounts of the ways in which their personal worldviews affect how they respond to science, religion and the environment.

Links and resources

Go to **www.natre.org.uk/bqic-challenging-knowledge-in-re** for full links and references for this section.

Our thanks to Dr Alexander Hall for writing the scenarios, for supporting the Prophet Attenborough pages, and for his advice throughout. For a fascinating general introduction to this topic, read: Alexander Hall, 'A Humanist Blockbuster? Jacob Bronowski and The Ascent of Man', in *Rethinking History, Science, and Religion: An Exploration of Conflict and the Complexity Principle*, ed. Bernard Lightman (Pittsburgh, PA: University of Pittsburgh Press, 2019).

TEACHING and learning CORE LEARNING

A What are the natural sciences, and what do scientists do?

Use the investigator file (Chapter 8 on pp. 22–23) to introduce the disciplines of natural sciences illustrated through a focus on environmental science. Give students the interview questions and answers separately, for them to match the answers to the questions. Explore the key features. Refer to this investigator file during the remaining activities.

8 Investigator FILES

Introducing natural sciences

Using natural sciences to investigate the ENVIRONMENT

pp. 22–23

B Role-playing real life: rising sea levels

- Resource 9.1 (p. 28) introduces an example of a real impact as a result of climate change. Read the information on p. 28 and set up the scenario. Put students into groups of six, using the role cards (Resource 9.2 online). (NB students should make use of their theological study of Genesis from previous chapters to inform these discussions.) Give them time to discuss possible courses of action and agree the parish council's decision, giving their reasons.
- Each group gives feedback on their decisions and their reasons. Discuss any differences of opinion and the reasons behind them.
- Reflect on the process. Ask students to rank the most influential voices in the exercise, and compare that ranking with their own rankings as to who should have most influence. Note that although the scientists can describe the situation, the decisions for action go beyond the data.
- Ask students to comment on and explain the relative influence of the environmental scientists and the religious communities. If this were a coastal village in Bangladesh rather than northern England, what might be different?
- Read the Reflections section on p. 29 together. Ask students to identify at least three ways in which religious perspectives contribute to (a) this specific debate, and (b) the wider climate change debate.

C Startling imagery: world under water

For an opportunity to reflect further on some of the matters raised in Activity B, Resource 9.3 (online) provides some images created by Nikolay Lamm, showing Florida and London under water, assuming the rise of sea levels predicted by scientists as a result of a 2-degree rise in global temperatures. Use the images and reflect on the huge challenges that potentially face the world – in even the wealthiest nations. Look at the Climate Central Surging Seas site, and explore the data for coastal areas in the UK and beyond. What are the implications for the UK and the wider world? Additional weblinks are given on: **www.natre.org.uk/bqic-challenging-knowledge-in-re**

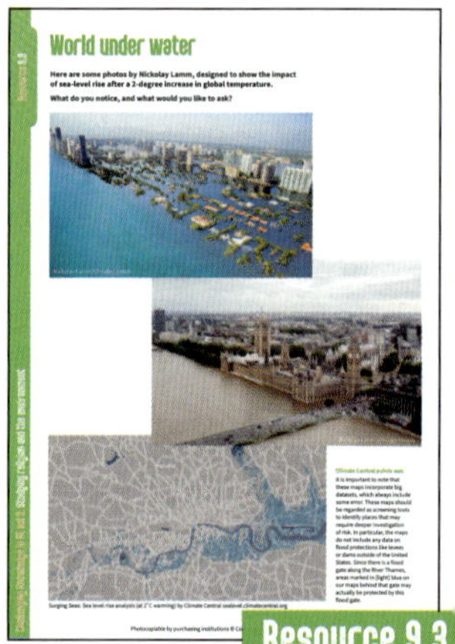
World under water

Resource 9.3

D The Anthropocene: a human-centred world

You may like to give your students an additional opportunity to explore some key implications from the findings of environmental science, using Resource 9.4 (pp. 30–31) to learn about the idea of the Anthropocene epoch. This is a proposal from geologists to acknowledge that the last epoch has come to an end (12,000 years of the Holocene age, from the last ice age to today) – and that catastrophic climate change is a result of human devastation. The age is now human-centred, hence the name Anthropocene (from the Greek *anthropos*, 'humanity'). Read the background information and set up students to consider the questions around when the 'human-centred' age began. Give them the three perspectives offered – and add one or two more, as reflected in your local area.

After group feedback, ask the students to look at the Reflections section on p. 31. Consider the contribution of religious traditions (see also the examples on Resource 3.2 online and pp. 20–21. Students should draw on their earlier learning from theological perspectives here.). How consistent is the idea of the Anthropocene with the worldviews of these traditions? How important are humans? How important is the natural world? What forms of wisdom do non-religious worldviews offer on this?

E Implications: some challenging questions

Ask students to raise any questions they have about the relationship between humans and the environment, in the context of religious and non-religious worldviews, theology and environmental science. If necessary, categorise their questions into those that might be answerable by theology, ethics or environmental science. Select the religious/theological or moral questions that get them most engaged, and discuss them. See Resource 9.5 (online) for some examples to debate.

Humans and the environment: some challenging questions

Resource 9.5

F Reflecting on values and personal worldviews

Ask students to reflect on some core human values such as justice, equality, freedom, human rights and responsibilities, love, service, compassion etc. Some religious traditions might add sanctity of life, *ahimsa*, or stewardship. How important are these values within religious and non-religious worldviews? How do they relate to our responses to the natural world and our place in it? Use a target board for students to consider how central these values are to themselves, and then talk about what practical difference these values make in their lives. What has influenced their thinking? How do these ideas affect their way of seeing and responding to the world (their personal worldviews)? What actions might they take in response to what they have been learning about humans and the environment?

TEACHING AND LEARNING: DIGGING DEEPER

G 'Prophet Attenborough' and the scientific blockbuster

Use pp. 32–33 to explore ways in which popular environmental documentaries on television can both absorb biblical prophetic tropes and present science / natural history in a religious way. Additional links, content and ideas are available on Resource 10.1 online. Encourage students to use the idea of 'religious' and 'secular' portrayals of science as lenses through which to examine these kinds of TV shows. You could ask them to respond to one or more of the following statements, by drawing on their learning then offering a critical analysis and thoughtful personal response:

- Science documentaries play a prophetic role in today's society.
- Science today has taken a role of religion in offering certainty.
- If the prophet Amos were alive today, he would be hosting nature documentaries and warning humanity.
- Without God we tend to start worshipping ourselves. (Jonathan Sacks)
- Many popular scientists are atheists, but they use religious language and cast themselves as priests. (Eliane Glaser)

H Drawing things together

This unit explores how science works to inform our understanding of the world but does not dictate our choices about how to act. This book looks at both theology and natural sciences.

Ask students to consider the value of both science and theology in helping us to make choices in relation to the natural world:

- How might the discipline of science be helpful when choosing an action that affects the environment?
- How might the discipline of theology be helpful when choosing an action that affects the environment?
- If your answers to both the above are positive, then how might using both theology and environmental science together help people to be good stewards when making decisions about actions that affect the natural world?
- How can these two disciplinary communities work together as we face this challenge?

Scenario 1: What would you do as sea levels rise? Who decides?

Findings in environmental science can indicate complex problems. The data only takes us so far, however. To make a decision about *if*, *when* and *how* to act requires people to balance a range of needs, and draw on different ways of thinking. The situation raises practical, human, financial, political and ethical problems, for example. Work in a group, taking roles in this scenario, to explore both the data and the challenge of deciding how to act.

The big picture: rising sea levels

Governments, scientists and communities around the world continue to try to find solutions to reduce our global greenhouse gas emissions. To lessen the effects of human-caused climate change, this needs to be done on a large scale. However, even if we stopped all fossil fuel emissions tomorrow, there are climatic changes already under way that are affecting communities across the globe.

Coastal communities in particular are vulnerable to the effects of climate change:

a. global average sea levels are predicted to rise by about 24–30 cm by the year 2065 and by at least 40–63 cm by 2100
b. coastal storms are set to increase in frequency and strength
c. low-lying island nations and coastal countries, such as the Solomon Islands and Bangladesh, are already losing large amounts of land to encroaching salt water
d. parts of wealthier island nations such as the United Kingdom are also under serious threat from rising sea levels.

Many experts are already working on ways to adapt our societies to cope with these new challenges. Environmental scientists continue to collect data, model different future pathways, and work with experts from the social sciences, such as economists. However, addressing the climate crisis requires the input of everyone in society. Scientists can only outline the problem and predict possible future issues. Making difficult moral, ethical, financial and political decisions on how to reduce the harm and adapt to the worst effects of climate change requires input from leaders (religious as well as secular), artists, charities, community groups – and *you*!

The local situation: towns under threat

To help manage the threat posed by sea-level rise there are several approaches and tools available. More traditional hard engineering approaches, such as walls to protect against the sea, are very expensive. They also have to be balanced with natural solutions, such as making more space for natural habitats like salt marshes, which can take on extra seawater when flooding occurs, reducing the damage to the land.

While the scientific data on the threat facing many coastal communities in the UK is clear, what should be done to protect these communities can only be answered satisfactorily by including political, financial, moral and ethical considerations. For example:

- Should the national government fund physical flood defences at whatever cost to save historic villages?
- Should natural processes be allowed to take over?
- If they do, should the community members be left to fend for themselves, or should they receive compensation (if so, where from?) to help them rebuild their lives elsewhere?

The scenario: delay, defend or retreat?

You are all members of a fictional village on the north-east coast of England, which is under threat from rising sea levels. The British government has informed the parish council that it will not continue to fund sea defences for the historic village centre. You only have enough budget to either:

- maintain the current sea defences, which means that for now all of the community will be safe, but in

20–25 years the sea will regularly breach the defences and the whole village may have to be abandoned, *or*

- build new, higher defences to protect the historic centre. Unfortunately, a side-effect of these higher defences will be more flooding to a business park on the edge of the village. You do not have the budget to pay these businesses any compensation, *or*
- begin a managed retreat, rebuilding the most at-risk buildings further inland on higher ground, and allowing the historic centre of the village to become a wild salt marsh again.

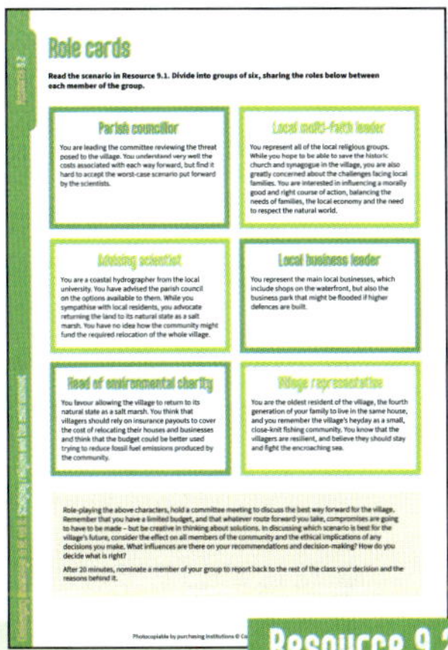

Resource 9.2

Divide into groups of six, sharing the roles below between each member of the group. Use Resource 9.2 (online) for more detail on each role.

The roles

- **Parish councillor**
- **Local multi-faith leader**
- **Advising scientist**
- **Local business leader**
- **Head of environmental charity**
- **Village representative**

Role-playing the above characters, hold a committee meeting to discuss the best way forward for the village. Remember that you have a limited budget, so whichever route forward you take compromises are going to have to be made – but be creative in thinking about solutions.

In discussing which scenario is best for the village's future, consider the effect on all members of the community and the ethical implications of any decisions you make. What influences are there on your recommendations and decision-making? How do you decide what is right?

After 20 minutes, nominate a member of your group to report to the rest of the class your decision and the reasons behind it.

Reflections

There is no single correct answer to the difficult scenario facing the villagers. Hopefully in your discussions you considered the different needs of fellow villagers, whether protecting historic buildings and businesses should take precedence over the natural environment, and how the difficulties of this one village are connected to other villages all over the world.

Over the coming decades, climate change, caused primarily by the fossil fuel emissions of wealthier nations like the UK, is going to affect some communities much worse than others. So we are going to have to take difficult decisions and make compromises with regard to how we deal with the challenges facing us.

In his circular letter entitled *Laudato si': On Care for our Common Home* (© Libreria Editrice Vaticana), Pope Francis, the head of the Roman Catholic Church, argued:

> The poorest areas and countries are less capable of adopting new models for reducing environmental impact because they lack the wherewithal to develop the necessary processes and to cover their costs. We must continue to be aware that, regarding climate change, there are differentiated responsibilities. As the United States bishops have said, greater attention must be given to 'the needs of the poor, the weak and the vulnerable, in a debate often dominated by more powerful interests'. We need to strengthen the conviction that we are one single human family. There are no frontiers or barriers, political or social, behind which we can hide, still less is there room for the globalization of indifference.
>
> Pope Francis, 2015

The Dalai Lama, spiritual leader of Tibetan Buddhists, has also advocated solutions to the climate crisis that involve bringing people together and prioritising the needs of communities and nature above those of business and profit:

> Over-exploitation of our natural resources results from ignorance and greed, and a lack of respect for life on Earth. Saving the world from the climate crisis is our common responsibility.
>
> The Dalai Lama, 2020

Our only home: a climate change appeal to the world by The Dalai Lama and Franz Alt (Bloomsbury)

Extensive links to further relevant resources can be found at **www.natre.org.uk/bqic-challenging-knowledge-in-re**

Resource 9.4

Scenario 2: Surviving the Anthropocene age: will life on Earth make it?

As well as triggering climate change by our greenhouse gas emissions, humans are also damaging many other parts of the natural world on a scale not seen before in our species' history. Environmental scientists have repeatedly warned us that from plastic pollution to the mass extinction of species because of habitat loss, humans are pushing the limits of what the Earth's natural systems can cope with.

The situation: human impact

To help sum up the sheer scale of human influence on the Earth, scientists have begun using a new term to describe the era we live in, the *Anthropocene*. It comes from the Ancient Greek words for 'human' and 'new'. Scientists use the term to argue that the Earth is entering a new period in its geological history: for the first time ever, humanity has become the primary driver of changes to the planet.

Environmental scientists can measure these changes using many different techniques and methods. These range:

- from the microscopic (e.g. biologists who measure the uptake of microplastics in fish)
- to the global (e.g. satellite imagery shows that despite slowing rates, humans are still cutting down an area of forest almost the size of England every year).

The data compiled and analysed by environmental scientists shows that humans are affecting nearly every aspect of the natural world in alarming ways.

Environmental scientists can alert us to the scale and urgency of many issues, but it takes the input of many different experts and a wide range of members of society to agree on the best course of action to solve these major environmental problems. As a result, many scientists, as well as economists, historians and theologians have quickly adopted the concept of the Anthropocene.

Outstanding issues

Geologists call the time from the end of the last ice age (around 12,000 years ago) the Holocene. Some geologists have proposed the Anthropocene as a new geological epoch, although it has not been officially adopted by geologists. There is much debate about when we should say the Anthropocene began:

- should it be during the Industrial Revolution of the 1800s, when we began burning fossil fuels on a scale that, as we found out years later, would alter the atmosphere?
- or should it be as long ago as 8,000 years ago, when we started altering our landscapes to farm crops?

This ongoing disagreement about when exactly the Anthropocene began points us to some of the other limitations of this term:

+ It is a useful concept for scientists trying to assess the scale of human impacts on the Earth.
+ It has also been an important tool in helping to alert the rest of society to the urgency of the situation.
+ It highlights how all humans are connected.
− Some experts in the humanities warn that the term covers up the huge inequalities that exist within societies, and between different countries, both historically and today, such as:
  - it ignores how major issues such as racism and poverty have affected environmental damage
  - it ignores how wealthier nations have overwhelmingly caused many of the issues we face today.

Thinking things through: different perspectives

Split into groups of three. Consider and discuss the three points below.

For each, put yourselves in the shoes of different people in society. How might your perspective change if you were:

a. the boss of an oil company?
b. the leader of a Hindu or Muslim or Christian community in a drought-affected region of the world?
c. the leader of an environmental charity based in London looking to help poorer drought-affected regions in other parts of the world?

- When did the Anthropocene begin? When do you think humans began altering the Earth on a global scale? Do you think that modern environmental activities (e.g. clearing rainforests for beef farming) should be considered as different from historic practices (e.g. clearing those forests for homesteads and smallholdings)? If so, why? (E.g. scale, complexity, speed etc.)

- If humans are now changing the world on a global scale, where do you think the responsibility for the addressing these problems primarily lies? (E.g. individuals, wealthy nations, everyone, big business etc.)
- Where solutions to individual environmental issues can be found, do you think:

a. we should prioritise the solutions that simply encourage leaving the natural systems alone?
b. we should interfere, but minimally?
c. we should use cutting-edge technologies to fix ecosystems?

For example, in attempting to reduce the amount of carbon dioxide in the atmosphere, do you think we should prioritise (b) planting more trees, or (c) developing carbon capturing technologies that can absorb much more carbon dioxide than an individual tree? Or … something else?

Reflections

The concept of the Anthropocene is useful for bringing together the huge amount of data and scientific research which shows that humans are having an unprecedented and unsustainable effect on the natural world. However, the term and the scientific data it represents do not provide our societies with the answers to how we can best go about making the changes needed to avoid complete environmental collapse. Your discussions have hopefully already raised some of the ethical and moral questions related to our responsibility – both as individuals and as a society – for protecting the natural world that we humans rely on.

For centuries many major religions and belief systems have taught about our moral responsibilities with regard to the natural world. The quotes below offer some positions advocated by a few major worldviews:

A Christian perspective

One of the buzzwords of recent years has been 'sustainability' … But what the word points to is the sense of obligation to hand on to our children and grandchildren a legacy that helps them live and flourish. Building to last is something we all understand. … A lot of the time we just don't let ourselves think about the future with realism. A culture of vast material waste and emotional short-termism is a culture that is a lot more fragile than it knows. How much investment are we going to put in towards a safer and more balanced future? A big question. But too big to avoid. And, if we feel a bit paralysed by just how big it is, well, we can at least start by a visit this week to the nearest recycling bins.

Former Archbishop of Canterbury
Rowan Williams, 2007

Archbishop of Canterbury's New Year message for 2008 (BBC)

A Muslim perspective

Our species, though selected to be a caretaker or steward (*khalīfah*) on the earth, has been the cause of such corruption and devastation on it that we are in danger of ending life as we know it on our planet. This current rate of climate change cannot be sustained, and the earth's fine equilibrium (*mīzān*) may soon be lost. As we humans are woven into the fabric of the natural world, its gifts are for us to savour. But the same fossil fuels that helped us achieve most of the prosperity we see today are the main cause of climate change. Excessive pollution from fossil fuels threatens to destroy the gifts bestowed on us by God – gifts such as a functioning climate, healthy air to breathe, regular seasons, and living oceans. But our attitude to these gifts has been short-sighted, and we have abused them. What will future generations say of us, who leave them a degraded planet as our legacy? How will we face our Lord and Creator?

Islamic Declaration on
Global Climate Change

ifees.org.uk/about/islamic-declaration-on-global-climate-change

A secular Humanist perspective

Humanists are guided by reason and science and recognise a moral duty towards the welfare of our fellow beings and the natural world. Humanists seek to engage in dialogue and debate rationally, intelligently, and with evidence, and promote the belief that humans are part of a wider natural world which must be treated sustainably for the sake of current and future generations.

Humanists UK, 2021

humanism.org.uk/humanist-climate-action

Extensive links to further relevant resources can be found at **www.natre.org.uk/bqic-challenging-knowledge-in-re**

10 Prophet Attenborough and the scientific blockbuster

The role of the prophet in the Judaeo-Christian tradition was to communicate God's truth to people. Prophets warned people of the consequences of their behaviour when they chose to go their own way. Prophets offered hope and a vision for future peace and wholeness, if people lived in harmony with God.

For example, the prophet Amos warned against injustice and inequality (see Amos 8:4–10). Prophet Isaiah presented a vision of a future world of harmony between people and with nature (Isaiah 65:17–25).

This chapter asks you to consider whether science has taken on some of the prophetic roles of religion, and whether we have secular prophets who teach us scientific truth, warn us about our behaviour and offer a vision of hope of living in harmony with our planet.

Getting started: how do nature documentaries present their stories?

Dr Alexander Hall studies how science is presented in TV documentaries. He says that when making nature documentaries, filmmakers and producers make lots of decisions about what to film, how to tell the story they present, and what messages they want to get across to you, the viewer. Next time you watch a nature documentary ask yourself the following:

- Is there a presenter on screen, or is the programme just narrated by a voice whose owner you can't see?
- Does the programme just show pristine natural environments, or does it include other humans and urban spaces?
- Does the programme show the negative effects of human activities, such as pollution or habitat destruction?
- Does the narrator or presenter ask you, the viewer, to change your behaviour or your beliefs?

Image: Pictorial Press Ltd / Alamy Stock Photo

Stories and iconography in secular science documentaries

Humans are a storytelling species. Origin stories, parables, morality tales, new scientific discoveries – stories catch our attention and often communicate more than a list of facts. Nature documentaries tell a story, shaping a series of narratives: with the scene set, they introduce a disruption that means some challenge has to be overcome. They then show lots of effort, leading to a crunch point: will the protagonists survive? And then a resolution, one way or the other.

One famous example was in *Planet Earth II*, where an iguana hatchling is chased by racer snakes.

Watch some extracts (Resource 10.1 online) to see if you can see any parallels between biblical storytelling and the documentaries. For example:

- Wise person (older, male, white-haired … ?) passes on truth – pictured on a mountain-top with a halo of light behind
- The narrator uses superlatives: awesome, magnificent, wonderful etc. (e.g. Psalm 105)
- Mention of the vastness of the universe; or how small humans are in the larger scheme of global/cosmic processes (e.g. Psalm 8; Job 38–42)
- Images of Eden, a paradise of extraordinary richness, complexity, beauty and interrelatedness (e.g. Genesis 2)
- Recognition that humans are causing problems in this Eden (e.g. Genesis 3)
- Potential catastrophe awaits (e.g. six 'Woes!' in Isaiah 5:8–25)
- Calls for humans to act to change their ways (e.g. Amos 8)
- Visions of hope for a better future (e.g. Isaiah 65; Revelation 21)

See online Resource 10.2 to explore the impact of nature documentaries.